foreword

The First Nations cuisine of Canada is a tapestry of cultures. The bounty of the land, sea, lakes and rivers is reflected in the cooking customs of the people who lived from the earth. Smoked salmon, venison, bison, fiddleheads, wild rice, berries—Aboriginal peoples based their cuisine on foods that were readily available in their surroundings. The diversity of plants and animals throughout the regions of this country is featured in this small introduction to aboriginal recipes.

While the depth of First Nations cuisine deserves a lifetime of study drawn on the millennia of its evolution, these few select recipes represent a sampling of some of our favourites from across the country. The recipes are inspired by traditional native cooking, combining ingredients that were used historically with ingredients commonly available today. We've included brief descriptions of some of the history, culture and ingredients that are the foundation of the book.

wild mushroom soup with herb oil

In the wild mushroom world, morels are the greatest find for foragers. It was traditional to pinch them off, not dig them out of the ground, so more would grow to enjoy in future years. Because some mushrooms contain deadly toxins, eat only mushrooms positively identified as edible.

Fresh, cleaned wild mushrooms, such as morels or chanterelles	3 cups	750 mL
Olive oil	2 tbsp.	30 mL
Unsalted butter	2 tbsp.	30 mL
Unsalted butter	2 tbsp.	30 mL
Large yellow onion, diced	1	1
Large Yukon Gold potatoes, diced	2	2
Dry sherry	1/4 cup	60 mL
Bouquet garni of parsley, thyme and bay leaf (see Tip, page 64)	1	1
Dried juniper berries, bruised	3	3
Garlic cloves, minced	4	4
Chicken or vegetable stock	8 cups	2 L
Heavy cream	1 cup	250 mL
Herb oil	6 tbsp.	90 mL

Slice mushrooms into even-sized pieces. Heat olive oil and first amount of butter in large pot. Add mushrooms in batches and cook until nicely browned. Remove mushrooms and set aside.

In same pot, melt remaining butter. Add onions and potatoes. Cook until golden, then deglaze with sherry. Add bouquet garni, juniper berries, garlic, mushrooms and stock. Bring to a boil, then reduce heat to a simmer and cook until liquid is reduced by a third.

Stir in cream. Bring almost to a boil, then remove from heat. Remove bouquet garni. Puree soup in blender until smooth. Drizzle individual servings with herb oil. Serves 6.

1 cup (250 mL): 440 Calories; 34 g Total Fat (10 g Mono, 11 g Poly, 11 g Sat); 50 mg Cholesterol; 31 g Carbohydrates (3 g Fibre, 5 g Sugar); 5 g Protein; 830 mg Sodium

clam chowder

West coast Haida legend has it that raven discovered the first humans cowering naked and afraid in a huge clamshell he found on the beach. He coaxed them from the shell, and they became the first Haida.

Large potatoes, cubed	3	3
Large carrots, cut into 1 inch (2.5 cm) pieces	3	3
Bacon slices, diced	10	10
Large green pepper, diced	1	1
Chopped celery	1 1/2 cups	375 mL
Chopped onion	1 1/2 cups	375 mL
Cans of condensed cream of potato soup (10 oz., 284 mL, each)	2	2
Lemon pepper	1/4 tsp.	1 mL
Salt	1 tsp.	5 mL
Pepper	1/8 tsp.	0.5 mL
Cans of baby clams, drained, liquid reserved (5 oz., 142 g, each)	2	2
Canned stewed tomatoes (14 oz., 398 mL)	1	1
Milk	1 1/2 cups	375 mL

Cook potato and carrot in boiling water in large saucepan until tender. Do not drain.

Fry bacon until crisp. Remove to plate lined with paper towel to drain. Discard all but 1 tbsp. (15 mL) of fat.

Add green pepper, celery and onion to frying pan. Cook until soft. Add to potato mixture along with bits from pan. Stir in bacon, liquid from clams, potato soup, lemon pepper, salt and pepper. Simmer for 10 to 15 minutes.

Add clams, tomatoes and milk. Heat through, without boiling, to prevent curdling. Makes 20 cups (5 L) chowder.

1 cup (250 mL): 170 Calories; 9 g Total Fat (4 g Mono, 1 g Poly, 3 g Sat); 15 mg Cholesterol; 18 g Carbohydrates (2 g Fibre, 4 g Sugar); 5 g Protein; 620 mg Sodium

nettle soup

Stinging nettles are not only delicious in recipes, they have been used medicinally for centuries to treat allergies, arthritis, internal bleeding, kidney stones and urinary tract infections. Blanching the nettles removes their sting.

Salt	2 tsp.	10 mL
Fresh nettles	1 lb.	454 g
Olive oil	2 tbsp.	30 mL
Shallots, finely chopped	1/4 cup	60 mL
Onion, finely chopped	1/4 cup	60 mL
Garlic clove, minced	2	2
Celery, chopped	1/2 cup	125 mL
Potato, peeled and diced	1 lb.	454 g
Chicken broth	6 cups	1.5 L
Bay leaf	1	1
Thyme, chopped	1 tbsp.	15 mL
Cream	3 tbsp.	45 mL
Pepper	1/2 tsp.	2 mL
Salt	1/4 tsp.	1 mL
Hard boiled eggs, chopped	2	2

Add salt to large pot filled with water and bring to a boil. Add nettles and cook for 1 to 2 minutes, until softened. Transfer nettles into ice bath. Drain in colander. Trim off and discard any coarse stems, then roughly chop nettles.

In large pot, heat oil over medium. Add next 4 ingredients and cook until soft, about 5 minutes.

Add next 4 ingredients. Bring to a boil, then reduce heat and simmer for 15 minutes. Add nettles. If necessary, add enough water to cover nettles. Bring soup back to a simmer and cook until potatoes and nettles are tender, about 15 minutes.

Remove bay leaves. Puree soup in batches in blender (or use immersion blender). Return to pot. Stir in cream, salt and pepper. Garnish with chopped egg. Serves 4.

1 serving: 250 Calories; 9 g Total Fat (6 g Mono, 1 g Poly, 2.5 g Sat); 10 mg Cholesterol; 36 g Carbohydrates (10 g Fibre, 4 g Sugar); 27 g Protein; 1350 mg Sodium

seared scallops with mushrooms and leeks

Diving for Sakskalaas *or* sasgale, *as the east coast Mi'kmaq people call scallops, is a favourite activity on a hot July or August day.*

Leek, white and pale green parts only	1	1
Oyster mushrooms	2 cup	500 mL
Olive oil	1 tbsp.	15 mL
Large sea scallops, patted very dry	16	16
Salt, to taste		
Black pepper, to taste		
Fish or vegetable stock	2 cups	500 mL

Wash leek well and cut into 1 1/2 x 1/2 inch (3.8 x 12 mm) strips. Tear oyster mushrooms into strips.

Heat olive oil in large pan over high. Sprinkle scallops with salt and pepper. Quickly sear scallops to golden brown on both flat sides. Reduce heat to medium. Add leeks and mushrooms. Cook until just softened, about 1 or 2 minutes.

Add stock and simmer, uncovered, until scallops are just cooked through, about 4 to 8 minutes. Remove from heat. Divide leeks and mushrooms evenly among 4 soup plates. Nestle scallops on top and pour broth over. Serves 4.

1 serving: 280 Calories; 5 g Total Fat (2.5 g Mono, 1 g Poly, 0.5 g Sat); 80 mg Cholesterol; 12 g Carbohydrates (2 g Fibre, 1 g Sugar); 41 g Protein; 610 mg Sodium

mussels with white wine and garlic

Ancient shell middens—dating back 9000 years and containing mussel shells, clamshells, bones and other kitchen scraps piled to heights of 9 feet (2.75 m)—have been excavated on the west coast, a testament to First Peoples' love of, and dependence on, shellfish.

Mussels (see Tip, page 64)	4 lbs.	2 kg
White wine, such as Chardonnay	1 cup	250 mL
Garlic cloves, minced	4	4
Butter	1 tbsp.	15 mL
Chives, chopped	1/4 cup	60 mL

Scrub mussels under cool running water and remove any beards. Discard mussels that don't close when gently tapped.

Bring white wine and garlic to a boil in large pot. Add mussels. Cover and reduce heat, cooking for about 5 to 6 minutes. Discard any mussels that have not opened. With slotted spoon, transfer mussels into serving dishes.

Turn heat to high and bring remaining liquid to a boil. Cook for 2 to 3 minutes, until it has reduced slightly. Whisk in butter. Spoon sauce over mussels and sprinkle with chives. Serves 5.

1 serving: 370 Calories; 10 g Total Fat; (2.5 g Mono, 2.5 g Poly, 3 g Sat); 110 mg Cholesterol; 15 g Carbohydrates (0 g Fibre, 0 g Sugar); 43 g Protein; 1060 mg Sodium

baked oysters on the half shell

Northwest coastal people relied on the ocean for much of their food. Men were responsible for fishing, but it was the women's task to collect shellfish, like mussels, clams and oysters. For a more authentic Aboriginal twist, substitute dandelion greens or seaweed for the spinach.

Fresh oysters, shucked and left in half shell	24	24
Canola oil	1 tbsp.	15 mL
Bags of fresh spinach, washed and chopped (9 oz., 255 g, each)	6	6
Medium onions, finely chopped	2	2
Garlic cloves, finely minced	3	3
Béchamel sauce (see Tip, page 64)	2 cups	500 mL
Dry bread crumbs	2 cups	500 mL

Arrange oysters in half shells on rimmed baking sheet. Set aside.

Heat oil in frying pan and cook spinach, onion and garlic. Add béchamel sauce and mix well. Slowly sprinkle and stir in just enough bread crumbs until mixture thickens. Spoon mixture over oysters. Bake in 350°F (175°C) oven for 15 to 18 minutes. Remove from oven and transfer to serving platter. Serves 4.

1 serving: 560 Calories; 18 g Total Fat 4 g Mono, 4.5 g Poly, 6 g Sat); 100 mg Cholesterol; 68 g Carbohydrates (11 g Fibre, 5 g Sugar); 33 g Protein; 1110 mg Sodium

lake erie smelts

Smelts are found in the Atlantic and Pacific oceans and some freshwater lakes across the country, and they were eaten by many native peoples. One way First Peoples of the Pacific coast made dried fish more appealing was to serve it with oil. Eulachon, a type of smelt, contains so much oil during spawning, that, once dried, it can be burned like a candle, hence its common name candlefish.

All-purpose flour	1/2 cup	125 mL
Salt	1/2 tsp.	2 mL
Pepper	1/4 tsp.	1 mL
Large egg	1	1
Lemon juice	1 tbsp.	15 mL
Cracker crumbs	1/2 cup	125 mL
Grated Parmesan cheese	1/3 cup	75 mL
Smelts, cleaned and bones removed	2 lbs.	900 g
Canola or peanut oil, for frying	1/2 cup	125 mL

Mix flour, salt and pepper on plate.

Beat egg and lemon juice in bowl.

Mix cracker crumbs and Parmesan cheese on separate plate. Coat fish with flour mixture. Dip fish in egg mixture, then roll in cracker crumb mixture.

Heat oil in frying pan. Pan-fry fish. When golden brown on first side, turn and brown other side. Serves 6.

1 serving: 370 Calories; 18 g Total Fat (9 g Mono, 3.5 g Poly, 3.5 g Sat); 50 mg Cholesterol; 13 g Carbohydrates (0 g Fibre, 0 g Sugar); 40 g Protein; 390 mg Sodium

cedar-planked arctic char with maple butter

West coast people relied on salmon for food and cedar trees for shelter, while the Anishinabe of the east marked the arrival of spring with a ceremony under the largest of maple trees.

Butter	1/2 lb.	250 g
Pure maple syrup	1/4 cup	60 mL
Chopped fresh thyme	1 tbsp.	15 mL
Fresh lemon juice	1 tbsp.	15 mL
Salt, to taste		
Pepper, to taste		
Untreated, rough cedar planks 1 ft (30 cm) long	2	2
Arctic char fillets (8 oz, 250 g, each)	5	5
Salt, to taste		
Pepper, to taste		

For maple butter, whip butter in stand mixer until fluffy and pale.

Mix next 5 ingredients together in separate bowl. Slowly add to butter. Continue to whip until butter is well combined. Dollop onto plastic wrap. Roll into cylinder and twist ends of wrap. Refrigerate.

Preheat barbecue to medium to medium-high and have a mister or pitcher of water standing by (in addition to a pail of water). Put planks right on barbecue. Put fillets on planks. Close lid of barbecue.

After 10 minutes, raise lid to see how fish is doing. Planks should be smoking and may even be burning. If they are, douse flames with a little water. It is okay for boards to burn a little. Close lid and check frequently for about 5 to 10 minutes more until done. Season with salt and pepper, and serve topped with a thin slice of maple butter. Do not save board to reuse. Serves 5.

1 serving: 540 Calories; 33 g Total Fat (3 g Mono, 0 g Poly, 8 g Sat); 80 mg Cholesterol; 5 g Carbohydrates (0 g Fibre, 3 g Sugar); 57 g Protein; 290 mg Sodium

stuffed ouananiche

Ouananiche, pronounced "wananish," is the Montagnais word for the unique landlocked salmon found in Labrador and Newfoundland fresh waters. The word means "he who is everywhere" or "the little lost."

Butter (or hard margarine)	2 tbsp.	30 mL
Sliced mushrooms	1 cup	250 mL
Shallots, sliced	2	2
Garlic cloves, minced	2	2
Dry bread crumbs	1 1/2 cups	375 mL
Bacon slices, cooked and crumbled	4	4
Pepper	1/2 tsp.	2 mL
Atlantic salmon (2 lbs., 900 g) cleaned, with head and tail removed	1	1
Salt, to taste		
Pepper, to taste		
Lemon wedges	4	4

Grease baking pan and set aside. Heat butter in medium frying pan and cook mushrooms, shallots and garlic. Mix in bread crumbs, bacon and pepper.

Press mixture into salmon cavity and season fish with salt and pepper. Place stuffed fish in prepared baking pan. Bake, covered, in 400°F (200°C) oven for about 30 minutes. Remove cover and bake for another 10 minutes, until fish flakes with a fork. Serve with lemon wedges. Serves 4.

1 serving: 720 Calories; 39 g Total Fat (14 g Mono, 9 g Poly, 12 g Sat); 165 mg Cholesterol; 32 g Carbohydrates (2 g Fibre, 3 g Sugar); 56 g Protein; 760 mg Sodium

salmon with blueberry lavender reduction

Lavender arrived in North America with the earliest European settlers and made its way into First Peoples' healing practices. The delicate purple blossoms of lavender are considered a symbol of cleanliness and purity. First Peoples used its essence to calm the mind.

Cooking oil	1 tbsp.	15 mL
Fresh blueberries,	1 cup	250 mL
Champagne vinegar	1 cup	250 mL
Granulated sugar	3/4 cup	175 mL
Dried lavender	1/2 tsp.	2 mL
Salt	1/4 tsp	1 mL
Salmon fillets (6 oz, 170 g, each)	4	4
Salt, to taste		
Pepper, to taste		
Fresh blueberries, for garnish		
Lavender sprigs, for garnish		

Preheat grill to medium-high. Clean thoroughly with wire brush and grease with oil.

Combine blueberries, champagne vinegar, sugar, dried lavender and salt in small saucepan. Bring to a low simmer and cook until mixture is reduced by about half and coats back of spoon. Use wooden spoon to press sauce through fine-mesh sieve.

While sauce is reducing, cook fish. Season fillets with salt and pepper. Place on grill skin side up. Cook until thinnest edge becomes opaque, 3 to 5 minutes, depending on thickness. Slip long spatula under fillet from side, lifting entire fillet at once, to flip. If fillet sticks, leave it for another 30 seconds before trying again. Cook on second side only to brown outside, about 2 minutes more.

To serve, place fillets on a plate and spoon sauce around fillets and over top. Garnish with fresh blueberries and sprig of lavender. Serves 4.

1 serving: 470 Calories; 16 g Total Fat (4.5 g Mono, 8 g Poly, 2 g Sat); 110 mg Cholesterol; 41 g Carbohydrate (trace Fibre, 40 g Sugar); 40 g Protein; 250 mg Sodium

smoked salmon

First Peoples smoked salmon to preserve it, but when fish is processed this way, the taste is exquisite. You can use any type of wood to perfume the salmon, as long as it is a hardwood. Stay away from pine and softwoods—the smoke they create is not pleasant.

Brown sugar	1/4 cup	60 mL
Kosher salt	1/4 cup	60 mL
Chopped rosemary	1 tsp.	5 mL
Salmon fillet (1 lb, 500 g)	1	1
Apple wood chips	1 cup	250 mL

Mix first 3 ingredients together in small bowl. Set aside. Lay down 2 pieces of plastic wrap, making sure they overlap. Spread half of mixture on wrap, and place salmon, skin side down, on top. Spread remaining mixture over salmon, making sure fish is completely covered. Wrap salmon in plastic wrap. Place on baking sheet and refrigerate for 4 hours, flipping once. Remove fish, rinse well and pat dry.

Preheat one side of barbecue to medium. Place wood chips in centre of square sheet of heavy foil. Bring corners together to make a pouch, and poke several holes in foil. Place over lit burner of barbecue. When smoke starts appearing from foil pouch, move salmon to unlit side of barbecue. Maintain temperature at no higher than 300°F (150°C). Cook until fish reaches an internal temperature of 140°F (60°C). Remove to a platter and serve immediately, or chill and serve later. Serves 8 as an appetizer.

1 serving: 90 Calories; 3.5 g Total Fat (1 g Mono, 1.5 g Poly, 0 g Sat); 30 mg Cholesterol; 3 g Carbohydrates (0 g Fibre, 3 g Sugar); 11 g Protein; 1630 mg Sodium

smoky trout burgers

First Peoples relied on fish not only for food but also for trade. In Ontario, lake trout, called tuladi *by the Ojibwe and* namayeush *by the Cree, was one of the most important items traded by First Peoples to early European explorers and settlers.*

Potatoes, cut into chunks	2	2
Smoked trout fillets, flaked	12 oz.	340 g
Creamed horseradish	2 tsp.	10 mL
Shallots, finely chopped	6	6
Grated zucchini, squeezed dry	3/4 cup	175 mL
Salt, to taste		
Pepper, to taste		
All-purpose flour	2 tbsp.	30 mL
Lean bacon slices	8	8

Boil potatoes in lightly salted water until cooked. Drain, mash and transfer to large bowl. Add trout, horseradish, shallots, zucchini, salt and pepper. Mix well. Separate mixture into 4 equal portions and form into patties. Refrigerate for 1 hour.

Preheat barbecue to medium-high. Dredge patties in flour and wrap each in 2 slices of bacon. Grill for 3 to 4 minutes on each side until golden. Makes 4 burgers.

1 burger: 640 Calories; 43 g Total Fat (19 g Mono, 6 g Poly, 13 g Sat); 95 mg Cholesterol; 27 g Carbohydrates (3 g Fibre, 2 g Sugar); 37 g Protein; 2640 mg Sodium

roasted duck with blueberry sauce

Migratory waterfowl was an important food source for the Cree, especially when geese and ducks became flightless during the summer breeding season and were easy to hunt.

Whole duck	1	1
Duck or chicken stock	4 cups	1 L
Ground cinnamon	1 tbsp.	15 mL
Salt, to taste		
Pepper, to taste		
Olive oil	2 tbsp.	30 mL
Fresh thyme	1 tbsp.	15 mL
Medium shallots, chopped	2	2
Red wine	1/2 cup	125 mL
Red wine vinegar	1/2 cup	125 mL
Butter	1 oz.	28 g
Granulated sugar	2 oz.	57 g
Freshly squeezed orange juice	1 cup	250 mL
Demi-glace	1 cup	250 mL
Fresh blueberry puree	6 tbsp.	90 mL
Blueberries, for garnish	50	50

Debone duck and leave legs whole. Brown legs in hot pan and cover with duck stock. Braise in 300°F (150°C) oven for 3 hours.

Score fat on breast in crisscross pattern so fat will render and leave crispy skin. Season duck with cinnamon, salt, pepper, oil and thyme and let stand for 1 hour. Increase oven temperature to 400°F (200°C). Sear duck breast in hot pan over medium, then place in oven for 7 to 10 minutes. Set aside to rest for 5 minutes so it reabsorbs its juices.

For the sauce, brown shallots in saucepan. Add wine and reduce by three-quarters. Add vinegar and reduce by three-quarters once more.

In a second saucepan, combine butter and sugar. Add orange juice and simmer until sugar is dissolved. Add shallot mixture, demi-glace and blueberry puree. Bring to a boil and strain. To serve, place whole berries in sauce for garnish. Serve duck topped with blueberry sauce. Serves 4.

1 serving: 1580 Calories; 140 g Total Fat (66 g Mono, 17 g Poly, 46 g Sat); 255 mg Cholesterol; 35 g Carbohydrates (2 g Fibre, 19 g Sugar); 39 g Protein; 1210 mg Sodium

partridge stew

Partridges are Old World birds and are not native to North America, but many people use the term to refer to grouse. Six grouse species are native to Canada and, depending on the species, can be found in grasslands, boreal forest or tundra throughout the country. They were an important food source for many First Peoples, especially when big game was scarce.

Grouse breasts, rinsed and patted dry	4	4
Water	4 cups	1 L
Chopped onions	1 cup	250 mL
Chopped carrots	2 cups	500 mL
Chopped onion	1 cup	250 mL
Water	2 cups	500 mL
Rice	1 1/2 cups	375 mL

Salt, to taste
Pepper, to taste

Place grouse breasts and first amount of water and onion in saucepan. Bring to a boil. Reduce heat and simmer for 2 hours.

With slotted spoon, remove grouse from pot. Remove meat from bones. Chop meat into small pieces and return to pot. Add carrots, remaining onion, remaining water and rice. Cover and simmer for about 20 minutes, until carrots are tender and rice is cooked.

Stir in salt and pepper and serve. Serves 4.

1 serving: 300 Calories; 6 g Total Fat (2 g Mono, 1 g Poly, 2 g Sat); 105 mg Cholesterol; 13 g Carbohydrates; 2 g Fibre; 7 g Sugar; 46 g Protein; 260 mg Sodium

goose burgers

Traditionally, James Bay Cree slowly roasted whole birds beside an open fire, hanging them from a string and twirling them constantly with a stick, the sigabon *way. The precious grease, used for medicinal purposes to ease congestion and as a cough syrup, was collected in a container below as the goose cooked.*

Ground goose breast	1 lb.	454 g
Italian dressing	1/3 cup	75 mL
Pepper	1/4 tsp.	1 mL
All-purpose flour	1 cup	250 mL
Salt	1/2 tsp.	2 mL
Pepper	1/4 tsp.	1 mL
Garlic powder	1/4 tsp.	1 mL
Vegetable oil	3 tbsp.	45 mL
Hamburger buns	4	4

In large bowl, mix together ground goose, Italian dressing and first amount of pepper. Refrigerate for at least 1 hour.

In small bowl, mix together flour, salt, remaining pepper and garlic powder. Spread out flour mixture on sheet of wax paper. Form goose mixture into 4 equal balls. Flatten 1 ball into patty on flour mixture. Flip over and coat other side. Repeat for other 3 balls.

Heat oil in frying pan over medium. Fry patties for about 10 minutes, flipping once or twice, until well cooked. Serve on hamburger buns with your favourite toppings. Makes 4 burgers.

1 burger: 530 Calories; 22 g Total Fat (9 g Mono, 4.5 g Poly, 4.5 g Sat); 95 mg Cholesterol; 48 g Carbohydrates (2 g Fibre, 5 g Sugar); 33 g Protein; 920 mg Sodium

venison jerky

Venison doesn't just refer to deer; the category includes all meat from the Cervidae family, including elk, moose and caribou. Drying the meat as we do in this recipe takes away the gamey taste.

Vegetable oil	3 tbsp.	45 mL
Venison, cut into 1/4 inch (6 mm) strips	2 lbs.	900 g
Salt	1 tsp.	5 mL
Pepper	1 tsp.	5 mL
Worcestershire sauce	2 tbsp.	30 mL
Soy sauce	2 tbsp.	30 mL
Garlic cloves, minced	2	2
Brown sugar	3 tbsp.	45 mL
Cayenne pepper	2 tsp.	10 mL
Molasses	2 tbsp.	30 mL
Water	1 cup	250 mL

Heat oil in frying pan. Add venison and season with salt and pepper. Cook until browned. Set aside to cool.

Combine remaining ingredients in large bowl. Add venison. Cover and refrigerate overnight. Remove venison strips from marinade with tongs and shake off excess liquid. Lay venison strips on large baking sheet and place in 175°F (80°C) oven for 2 1/2 hours. Turn strips over and place back in oven for 30 minutes with door propped open 2 to 3 inches (5 to 7.5 cm). The low temperature and door propped open allows the meat to dry out and cure completely. Makes about 2/3 lb. (300 g) jerky. Serves 10.

1 serving: 200 Calories; 7 g Total Fat (3.5 g Mono, 1.5 g Poly, 1.5 g Sat); 100 mg Cholesterol; 4 g Carbohydrates (0 g Fibre, 3 g Sugar); 28 g Protein; 400 mg Sodium

racks of venison with blackberry glaze

Always trim off all the fat and membrane from deer and moose to eliminate the strong, wild taste, say Dene Elders. This dish is good with parsnips.

Red wine	6 tbsp.	90 mL
Grainy mustard	3 tbsp.	45 mL
Shallot, minced	1	1
Crushed juniper	1 tsp.	5 mL
Rosemary stems	3	3
Blackberry preserve	7/8 cup	200 mL
Venison racks	3 lbs.	1.4 kg
Olive oil	2 tbsp.	30 mL
Salt, to taste		
Pepper, to taste		

Combine red wine, mustard, shallot, juniper and rosemary and reduce until slightly thickened. Add blackberry preserve and bring to a simmer. Remove from heat and set aside.

Brush venison with oil and season with salt and pepper. Heat a frying pan on high and sear all sides of venison racks, 1 rack at a time. Brush venison with half of blackberry glaze. Transfer seared racks to ovenproof pan and roast in 250°F (120°C) oven to 250°F (120°C) for 15 to 20 minutes until racks reach an internal temperature of 140°F (60°C). Once venison is cooked, brush on remaining glaze and let meat rest for 5 to 10 minutes to allow juices to settle before slicing. Serves 8.

1 serving: 320 Calories; 8 g Total Fat (3 g Mono, 1 g Poly, 1.5 g Sat); 30 mg Cholesterol; 25 g Carbohydrates (0 g Fibre, 21 g Sugar); 37 g Protein; 75 mg Sodium

grilled venison burgers

Ground venison is an updated way to serve this kind of wild meat.

Ground venison	2 lbs.	900 g
Salt	1/2 tsp.	2 mL
Pepper	1/2 tsp.	2 mL
Hamburger buns	8	8
Medium head of romaine lettuce, washed and torn	1	1
Medium red onion, thinly sliced	1	1
Fresh tomatoes, thinly sliced	2	2
Avocados, peeled and sliced	2	2
Cheddar cheese slices	8	8
Bacon, fried crisp	1 lb.	454 g

Form ground venison into 8 equal-sized patties and place on baking sheet. Season with salt and pepper. Preheat grill to medium and place patties on grill. Cook until desired doneness, about 4 to 5 minutes per side for medium-rare, longer for well done.

Put your cooked patties inside hamburger buns and top with lettuce, onion, tomato, avocado, cheese and bacon slices. Makes 8 burgers.

1 burger: 750 Calories; 49 g Total Fat (18 g Mono, 5 g Poly, 16 g Sat); 150 mg Cholesterol; 33 g Carbohydrates (6 g Fibre, 5 g Sugar); 43 g Protein; 1090 mg Sodium

tasty moose pie

On average, for a northern Aboriginal hunter, no kill could feed as many people as a moose (though a large bison could feed more). Amazing animals, moose can plunge to the bottom of lakes and remain there feeding for up to a full minute before bursting to the surface with fresh greens dangling from their mouth.

All-purpose flour	1 cup	250 mL
Baking powder	1 tsp.	5 mL
Salt	1/2 tsp.	2 mL
Shortening, cut into chunks	1/2 cup	125 mL
Mashed potatoes	1/2 cup	125 mL
Moose steak, cut into 1/4 inch (6 mm) strips	1 1/2 lbs.	680 g
Extra virgin olive oil	1/2 cup	125 mL
Salt	1 tsp.	5 mL
Pepper	1/2 tsp.	2 mL
Water	1 cup	250 mL

Sift together flour, baking powder and first amount of salt in bowl. Cut in shortening. Add mashed potato and mix to form a dough. Chill dough in refrigerator as you prepare meat.

Coat meat strips in olive oil and season with remaining salt and pepper. Roll up moose strips and place in large casserole dish. Add water. Cook, uncovered, in 300°F (150°C) oven for 1 hour. Roll dough out flat and place it over meat. Return casserole dish to oven and cook for another 20 minutes, until crust is golden brown. Let stand for 5 minutes before serving. Serves 6.

1 serving: 530 Calories; 38 g Total Fat (15 g Mono, 1.5 g Poly, 7 g Sat); 65 mg Cholesterol; 19 g Carbohydrates (trace Fibre, 0 g Sugar); 27 g Protein; 670 mg Sodium

roast bison with juniper berry gravy

Juniper is a "supermarket of the mountains" with a multitude of uses. You can season game with it to give the meat a tangy taste, and you can also use it to repel moths, soothe rheumatic pains and kill infectious germs.

Juniper berries	3 tbsp.	45 mL
Whole black peppercorns	2 tbsp.	30 mL
Whole cloves	4	4
Fennel seeds	1 tsp.	5 mL
Coriander seeds	1 tsp.	5 mL
Grape seed oil	1 tbsp.	15 mL
Bison sirloin roast (4 lb, 1.8 kg)	1	1
Salt	1 tbsp.	15 mL
Beef broth	1/2 cup	125 mL
Red wine	1/2 cup	125 mL
Water	1/2 cup	125 mL
Juniper berries, lightly crushed	1 tbsp.	15 mL
Cornstarch	2 tsp.	10 mL
Water	2 tbsp	30 mL
Balsamic vinegar	1 tbsp.	15 mL

Finely grind juniper berries, peppercorns, cloves, fennel seeds and coriander seeds in spice grinder. Lightly oil roast, sprinkle with salt, and rub with spice mixture. Heat large pan over medium-high. Sear roast to brown on all sides. Transfer to shallow roasting pan. Roast in 275°F (140°C) oven until internal temperature reaches 120°F (49°C) for rare, about 1 hour. Transfer to serving platter to rest, tented with foil, for at least 20 minutes before slicing.

For the gravy, add broth, wine, first amount of water and crushed juniper berries to roasting pan over medium-high heat. Simmer, stirring and scraping up brown bits, for 5 minutes. Strain through fine-mesh sieve into small saucepan over medium heat. Stir cornstarch into remaining water until dissolved, then add to mixture in small saucepan. Add balsamic vinegar. Simmer, whisking constantly, for 5 minutes. Serve alongside bison. Serves 8.

1 serving with 1/4 cup (60 mL) gravy: 300 Calories; 7 g Total Fat (2.5 g Mono, 2 g Poly, 2 g Sat); 160 mg Cholesterol; 3 g Carbohydrate (trace Fibre, trace Sugar); 49 g Protein; 1070 mg Sodium

cranberry bison meatballs

This recipe marries fruit and meat, much like the traditional survival food called pimmihkkan *(pimi means "grease" in Cree), which typically consisted of pounded meat, Saskatoon berries and grease to bind it together.*

Large egg, fork-beaten	1	1
Dried cranberries	1/4 cup	60 mL
Olive oil	2 tbsp.	30 mL
Ground allspice	1/2 tsp.	2 mL
Salt	1/2 tsp.	2 mL
Pepper	1/4 tsp.	1 mL
Medium ground bison	1 lb.	500 g
Canned whole cranberry sauce	1 cup	250 mL
Barbecue sauce	1/4 cup	60 mL
White vinegar	1 tsp.	5 mL
Pepper	1/4 tsp.	1 mL

Combine egg, cranberries, oil, allspice, salt and first amount of pepper in large bowl. Add bison and mix well. Roll into 3/4 inch (2 cm) balls. Arrange in single layer on greased baking sheet with sides. Cook in 375°F (190°C) oven for about 15 minutes until no longer pink inside.

For the glaze, combine cranberry sauce, barbecue sauce, vinegar and remaining pepper in medium frying pan. Heat and stir on medium until boiling. Add meatballs. Heat and stir for about 1 minute until glazed. Serves 7.

1 serving: 280 Calories; 15 g Total Fat (7 g Mono, 1 g Poly, 5 g Sat); 75 mg Cholesterol; 22 g Carbohydrates (0 g Fibre, 18 g Sugar); 13 g Protein; 340 mg Sodium

stuffed acorn squash

Squash is one of the three sacred sisters, along with corn and beans, of the Haudenosaunee (Mohawk). Corn served as the support for the beans, beans added nitrogen to the soil, and squash were planted between the garden rows to reduce the growth of weeds.

Acorn squash (1 1/2 lbs., 680 g)	1	1
Salt, to taste		
Pepper, to taste		
Dried cranberries	1/2 cup	125 mL
Hot water	1/4 cup	60 mL
Butter (or hard margarine)	3 tbsp.	45 mL
Chopped onion	1/4 cup	60 mL
Shiitake mushrooms	4 oz.	113 g
Chopped fresh sage	1 tsp.	5 mL
Chopped fresh thyme	1 tsp.	5 mL
Fresh (or frozen, thawed) kernel corn	1/2 cup	125 mL
Cooked assorted beans, such as cranberry beans and navy beans	1/2 cup	125 mL
Cooked wild rice	1/2 cup	125 mL

Remove top of squash by cutting circle about 2 inches (5 cm) in diameter around stem with sharp knife. Reserve lid. Scrape out and discard seeds and pulp. Sprinkle flesh with salt and pepper. Transfer to roasting pan.

Soften cranberries in hot water. Melt butter in large saucepan over medium heat. Add onion, mushrooms, sage and thyme. Pan-fry until beginning to soften, about 5 minutes. Stir in corn and cook for another 2 minutes. Remove from heat.

Add beans, wild rice and cranberries with their soaking liquid. Mound stuffing into squash cavity. Put lid on top of squash. Roast on middle rack of 425°F (220°C) oven until squash is tender and stuffing is heated through, about 45 minutes to 1 hour. Transfer to platter. To serve, scoop out a portion of stuffing along with some of the squash flesh.

1 serving: 550 Calories; 19 g Total Fat (4.5 g Mono, 1 g Poly, 11 g Sat); 45 mg Cholesterol; 91 g Carbohydrate (15 g Fibre, 34 g Sugar); 12 g Protein; 790 mg Sodium

pan-fried fiddleheads

Maliseet traditional wisdom holds that consuming fiddleheads helps cleanse the body of impurities and toxins. In addition to being high in fibre, fiddleheads are rich in iron, potassium, niacin, riboflavin, magnesium, zinc, phosphorus and vitamins A and C. A great way to clean fiddleheads of their papery, brown scales is to shake them in small batches in a paper bag.

Fresh fiddleheads	**1 lb.**	**500 g**
Unsalted butter	**1/3 cup**	**75 mL**
Lemon juice	**3 tbsp.**	**45 mL**
Salt, to taste		
Pepper, to taste		
Paprika, to taste		
Fine dry bread crumbs	**1/3 cup**	**75mL**

Clean fiddleheads well and cook in boiling, salted water for 5 to 7 minutes.

Melt butter in medium pan and add lemon juice, salt, pepper, paprika and bread crumbs. Toss hot fiddleheads in pan for another 3 to 5 minutes to coat well. Serves 5 as a side dish.

1 serving: 110 Calories; 10 g Total Fat (2.5 g Mono, 0 g Poly, 6 g Sat); 25 mg Cholesterol; 6 g Carbohydrates (0 g Fibre, 1 g Sugar); 4 g Protein; 110 mg Sodium

pickled sea asparagus

This salty green, which grows in tidal areas, was eaten raw or dried and ground for use in cakes and breads sweetened with honey by west coast nations like the Salish. In the photo, we've paired the sea asparagus with cucumber and grilled salmon.

Fresh sea asparagus	1 1/2 lbs.	750 g
Garlic cloves, peeled (optional)		
Water	1 1/2 cups	375 mL
White balsamic vinegar	1/2 cup	125 mL
Sugar	2/3 cup	150 mL
Kosher salt	2 tbsp.	30 mL
Mustard seeds	1 tsp.	5 mL
Pink peppercorns	1 tbsp.	15 mL
Fresh minced ginger	1/2 tsp.	2 mL

Blanch sea asparagus in boiling water for 5 to 10 seconds, then plunge into ice water to help leach out some saltiness. Pack drained asparagus into sterilized jars and add a few cloves of garlic to each, if using.

Bring remaining ingredients to a boil, and simmer for 15 minutes. Allow liquid to cool to room temperature, then pour over asparagus. Marinate in refrigerator at least 24 hours before serving. Keeps for 1 month in the refrigerator. Makes approximately four 8 oz. (250 mL) jars.

1 jar: 110 Calories; 0 g Total Fat; (0 g Mono, 0 g Poly, 0 g Sat); 0 mg Cholesterol; 24 g Carbohydrates (0 g Fibre, 19 g Sugar); 2 g Protein; 3690 mg Sodium

roasted jerusalem artichokes

Just as roasted potatoes have a richer flavour than boiled, roasting Jerusalem artichokes brings out the best taste in these tubers.

Garlic cloves, chopped	**4**	**4**
Extra virgin olive oil	**2 1/2 tbsp.**	**37 mL**
Jerusalem artichokes	**1 1/2 lbs.**	**680 g**
Salt, to taste		
Pepper, to taste		
Chopped fresh parsley	**1 tbsp.**	**15 mL**

Heat garlic and oil in small pot, and cook until garlic is soft.

Peel Jerusalem artichokes and cut into small chunks, placing chunks into bowl of acidulated water (see Tip, page 64) as you work. Put chokes in shallow roasting pan large enough to hold everything in a single layer comfortably. Strain garlic from oil and pour oil over chokes. Add salt and pepper and toss.

Bake in 350°F (175°C) oven for about 20 minutes, stirring once or twice, until tender. Sprinkle parsley over top and serve. Serves 4 as a side dish.

1 serving: 210 Calories; 9 g Total Fat (7 g Mono, 0.5 g Poly, 1.5 g Sat); 0 mg Cholesterol; 31 g Carbohydrates (3 g Fibre, 16 g Sugar); 4 g Protein; 75 mg Sodium

wild and white rice pilaf with dried cranberries

Wild rice was traditionally harvested in a canoe by bending the fruiting heads over the side of the canoe and hitting them with a stick, or shaking them, to dislodge the grains.

Butter (or hard margarine)	2 tbsp.	30 mL
Cipolline onions, julienned	1/3 cup	75 mL
Wild and white rice blend	1 cup	250 mL
Dried cranberries	1/2 cup	125 mL
Chopped fresh sage	1 tbsp.	15 mL
Salt	1/2 tsp.	2 mL
Water or broth	2 cups	500 mL

Melt butter in medium ovenproof saucepan on low heat. Add onions and pan-fry until softened, 1 to 2 minutes.

Add rice. Cook, stirring, until the grains of white rice become translucent, about 3 to 5 minutes.

Add dried cranberries, sage and salt. Pan-fry 1 minute more.

Add water or broth. Increase heat to medium-high and bring to a boil. Stir. Cover and transfer saucepan to oven. Cook in 350°F (175°C) oven for 45 minutes. Fluff with a fork before serving. Serves 5.

1 serving: 210 Calories; 5 g Total Fat (1.5 g Mono, 0 g Poly, 3 g Sat); 10 mg Cholesterol; 37 g Carbohydrate (2 g Fibre, 9 g Sugar); 4 g Protein; 400 mg Sodium

bannock

This is so much fun to make around the fire with friends and family. Be sure to whittle away the outer skin of your cooking stick to avoid the bitter taste of the bark. Try adding a handful of any of the following: chopped nuts, banana chips, dried fruit, cheese, cinnamon sugar, chocolate chips, seeds, fresh berries or whatever else you can come up with.

All-purpose flour	1 1/4 cups	310 mL
Baking powder	1 tbsp.	15 mL
Salt	1 tsp.	5 mL
Sugar	1 tbsp.	15 mL
Butter (or hard margarine)	3 tbsp.	45 mL
Large egg	1	1
Water	1/2 cup	125 mL
Cooking oil	1 tbsp.	15 mL

Combine flour, baking powder, salt and sugar in large bowl. Rub butter into flour mixture.

Combine egg and 1/4 cup (60 mL) water. Add to flour mixture, stirring to combine. Add enough of remaining water to make firm dough (you may not use the entire 1/2 cup, 125 mL). Knead dough for about 3 minutes. Let dough rest, covered, for 30 minutes.

Divide dough into quarters and shape each portion into ball. Flatten with rolling pin, or your hand, into disk about 1/2 inch (1 cm) thick. Heat frying pan over medium and add oil. Cook bannock on both sides, turning once, until golden brown. Alternatively, forego frying pan and simply twist dough evenly around a clean stick and hold over open campfire until golden and crispy. Makes 4 bannock.

1 bannock: 250 Calories; 10 g Total Fat (2.5 g Mono, 0.5 g Poly, 6 g Sat); 75 mg Cholesterol; 34 g Carbohydrates; 1 g Fibre; 3 g Sugar; 6 g Protein; 830 mg Sodium

basic cornmeal bread

Corn was a staple for the Huron Wendat of Ontario. It was pounded or ground into a coarse flour and made into unleavened bread that was cooked in hot ashes. Early settlers to Canada adopted this bread and added eggs, soured milk, baking soda and a sweetener, transforming it into the cornmeal bread we know today.

All-purpose flour	1 1/2 cups	375 mL
Yellow cornmeal	1 cup	250 mL
Granulated sugar	1/2 cup	125 mL
Baking powder	2 tsp.	10 mL
Baking soda	1 tsp.	5 mL
Salt	1/2 tsp.	2 mL
Large egg	1	1
Buttermilk (or soured milk, see Tip, page 64)	1 cup	250 mL
Butter (or hard margarine), melted	1/4 cup	60 mL

Measure first 6 ingredients into large bowl. Stir. Make a well in centre.

Combine remaining 3 ingredients in small bowl. Add to well. Stir until just moistened. Spread in greased 9 x 9 inch (23 x 23 cm) pan. Bake in 350°F (175°C) oven for about 30 minutes until wooden pick inserted in centre comes out clean. Let stand in pan for 5 minutes before removing to wire rack to cool. Cuts into 12 pieces.

1 piece: 190 Calories; 4.5 g Total Fat (1 g Mono, 0 g Poly, 2.5 g Sat); 30 mg Cholesterol; 32 g Carbohydrates (trace Fibre, 8 g Sugar); 3 g Protein; 300 mg Sodium

blueberry crisp

Blueberries are sacred to First Peoples because they can be dried and eaten during the long winter, and the blossom end of the berry is shaped like a five-pointed star, an indication the Creator sent the berries to relieve their children's hunger.

Fresh (or frozen) blueberries	4 cups	1 L
Honey	1/4 cup	60 mL
Lemon juice	2 tbsp.	30 mL
Lemon zest	2 tsp.	10 mL
Chopped fresh basil or mint	1/4 cup	60 mL
All-purpose flour	2 tbsp.	30 mL
Brown sugar	1/2 cup	125 mL
Rolled oats	1/2 cup	125 mL
All-purpose flour	1/2 cup	125 mL
Unsalted butter, softened	1/3 cup	75 mL
Ground cinnamon	1 tsp.	5 mL

Combine first 5 ingredients and pour into a buttered 6 cup (1.5 L) baking dish.

Combine remaining 6 ingredients in medium bowl and sprinkle over berry base. Bake in 375°F (190°C) oven for 25 to 30 minutes. Serve warm or at room temperature with ice cream or whipped cream. Serves 5.

1 serving: 400 Calories; 13 g Total Fat (3.5 g Mono, 1 g Poly, 8 g Sat); 35 mg Cholesterol; 70 g Carbohydrates (5 g Fibre, 46 g Sugar); 4 g Protein; 10 mg Sodium

saskatoon berry ice cream

Soapberries (soopolallies) were traditionally crushed, mixed with water and whipped up into "ice cream." To make soapberry ice cream, place 1 cup (250 mL) soapberries and 1 cup (250 mL) water in a wide-topped ceramic or glass mixing bowl. Do not use a plastic bowl or utensils, and make sure that nothing is greasy, or the berries will not whip properly. Whip the mixture with an electric eggbeater or hand whisk until it reaches the consistency of beaten egg whites. Gradually add 4 tbsp. (60 mL) sugar to the pink foam, but not too fast or the foam will "sink." Serve immediately. Even with sugar this treat will have a slightly bitter taste, but many people quickly grow to like it. Soapberries are not always readily available, so if a craving for ice cream strikes, try this saskatoon berry ice cream instead.

Whole milk	1 cup	250 mL
Heavy cream	3 cups	750 mL
Vanilla bean, split lengthwise	1	1
Egg yolks	5	5
Sugar	3/4 cup	175 mL
Saskatoon berries	2 1/2 cups	625 mL

In heavy-bottomed saucepan, heat milk, cream and vanilla bean until just before boiling, stirring occasionally. Remove from heat, take out vanilla bean, scrape out seeds and add them to milk. Set aside.

In mixing bowl, whisk egg yolks and sugar until pale yellow and thickened. Slowly pour about 1 cup (250 mL) of hot cream mixture into egg yolks, whisking constantly. Add yolk mixture back into remaining cream and cook over medium heat, stirring constantly, until mixture thickens and coats back of spoon. Do not let mixture boil at any time or it will curdle. Pour through fine-mesh strainer into bowl. Add saskatoon berries and freeze in ice cream maker according to manufacturer's instructions. Makes 4 cups.

***1/2 cup (125 mL):** 320 Calories; 21 g Total Fat (6 g Mono, 1 g Poly, 12 g Sat); 195 mg Cholesterol; 30 g Carbohydrates (2 g Fibre, 20 g Sugar); 4 g Protein; 40 mg Sodium*

recipe index

Acorn Squash, Stuffed, 44
Arctic Char, Cedar-planked, with
    Maple Butter, 16

Baked Oysters on the Half Shell, 12
Bannock, 54
Basic Cornmeal Bread, 56
Big Game
    Cranberry Bison Meatballs, 42
    Grilled Venison Burgers, 36
    Racks of Venison with Blackberry
        Glaze, 34
    Roast Bison with Juniper Berry
        Gravy, 40
    Tasty Moose Pie, 38
    Venison Jerky, 32
Bison, Roast, with Juniper Berry
    Gravy, 40
Blueberry Crisp, 58
Burgers
    Goose, 30
    Grilled Venison, 36
    Smoky Trout, 24

Cedar-planked Arctic Char with Maple
    Butter, 16
Clam Chowder, 4
Cornmeal Bread, Basic, 56
Cranberry Bison Meatballs, 42
Crisp, Blueberry, 58

Desserts & Snacks
    Bannock, 54
    Basic Cornmeal Bread, 56
    Blueberry Crisp, 58
    Saskatoon Berry Ice Cream, 60
Duck, Roasted, with Blueberry
    Sauce, 26

Fiddleheads, Pan-fried, 46
Fish & Seafood
    Baked Oysters on the Half Shell, 12
    Cedar-planked Arctic Char with
        Maple Butter, 16
    Lake Erie Smelts, 14
    Mussels with White Wine and
        Garlic, 10
    Salmon with Blueberry Lavender
        Reduction, 20
    Seared Scallops with Mushrooms
        and Leeks, 8
    Smoked Salmon, 22
    Smoky Trout Burgers, 24
    Stuffed Ouananiche, 18

Game Birds
    Goose Burgers, 30
    Partridge Stew, 28
    Roasted Duck with Blueberry
        Sauce, 26
Goose Burgers, 30
Grilled Venison Burgers, 36

Ice Cream, Saskatoon Berry, 60

Jerky, Venison, 32
Jerusalem Artichokes, Roasted, 50

Lake Erie Smelts, 14

Meatballs, Cranberry Bison, 42
Moose Pie, Tasty, 38
Mussels with White Wine and
    Garlic, 10

Nettle Soup, 6

Ouananiche, Stuffed, 18
Oysters, Baked, on the Half Shell, 12

Pan-fried Fiddleheads, 46
Partridge Stew, 28
Pickled Sea Asparagus, 48
Pilaf, Wild and White Rice, with Dried
    Cranberries, 52

Racks of Venison with Blackberry
    Glaze, 34
Roast Bison with Juniper Berry
    Gravy, 40
Roasted Duck with Blueberry
    Sauce, 26
Roasted Jerusalem Artichokes, 50

Salmon, Smoked, 22
Salmon with Blueberry Lavender
    Reduction, 20
Saskatoon Berry Ice Cream, 60
Scallops, Seared, with Mushrooms
    and Leeks, 8

Sea Asparagus, Pickled, 48
Seared Scallops with Mushrooms and
    Leeks, 8
Sides
    Bannock, 54
    Pan-fried Fiddleheads, 46
    Pickled Sea Asparagus, 48
    Roasted Jerusalem Artichokes, 50
    Wild and White Rice Pilaf with
        Dried Cranberries, 52
Smelts, Lake Erie, 14
Smoked Salmon, 22
Smoky Trout Burgers, 24
Soups & Stews
    Clam Chowder, 4
    Nettle Soup, 6
    Partridge Stew, 28
    Wild Mushroom Soup with
        Herb Oil, 2
Stuffed Acorn Squash, 44
Stuffed Ouananiche, 18

Tasty Moose Pie, 38

Venison Jerky, 32
Venison, Racks of, with Blackberry
    Glaze, 34

Wild and White Rice Pilaf with Dried
    Cranberries, 52
Wild Mushroom Soup with Herb Oil, 2

topical tips

Acidulated water: Acidulated water is just water to which a little acid—normally lemon or lime juice or vinegar—has been added; ½ tsp. (2 mL) per cup (250 mL) is enough. When you are peeling or cutting fruits or vegetables that discolour quickly when exposed to air, like apples, place them in acidulated water to prevent browning.

Béchamel sauce: To make Béchamel sauce, heat 2 tbsp. (30 mL) butter in a saucepan over low. Whisk in 2 tbsp. (30 mL) flour until smooth. Whisk in 1 1/4 cup (300 mL) milk. Season with salt and pepper.

Bouquet garni: To make a bouquet garni, wrap your herbs in cheesecloth and tie it shut to form a tidy bundle that can be easily extracted from the dish before serving.

Making soured milk: To make soured milk, measure 1 tbsp. (15 mL) white vinegar or lemon juice into a 1 cup (250 mL) liquid measure. Add enough milk to make 1 cup (250 mL). Stir. Let stand for 1 minute.

Storing mussels: Use your fresh mussels within 24 hours of purchasing them. Store fresh mussels in a colander and place the colander into a bowl. Cover the mussels with ice and then with a damp towel. The mussels will stay very cold and have good air circulation, without being submerged (or drowned) in water.

Nutrition Information Guidelines

Each recipe is analyzed using the Canadian Nutrient File from Health Canada, which is based on the United States Department of Agriculture (USDA) Nutrient Database.

- If more than one ingredient is listed (such as "butter or hard margarine"), or if a range is given (1 – 2 tsp., 5 – 10 mL), only the first ingredient or first amount is analyzed.

- For meat, poultry and fish, the serving size per person is based on the recommended 4 oz. (113 g) uncooked weight (without bone), which is 2 – 3 oz. (57 – 85 g) cooked weight (without bone)— approximately the size of a deck of playing cards.

- Milk used is 1% M.F. (milk fat), unless otherwise stated.

- Cooking oil used is canola oil, unless otherwise stated.

- Ingredients indicating "sprinkle," "optional" or "for garnish" are not included in the nutrition information.

- The fat in recipes and combination foods can vary greatly depending on the sources and types of fats used in each specific ingredient. For these reasons, the count of saturated, monounsaturated and polyunsaturated fats may not add up to the total fat content.